Previous Books by Thomas O'Grady

What Really Matters (2000)

Delivering the News (2019)

Coming Ashore

Ashore

New & Selected Poems

ARROWSMITH

Coming Ashore
New & Selected Poems
Thomas O'Grady

ISBN: 979-8-9915254-9-7

Boston — New York — San Francisco — Baghdad
San Juan — Kyiv — Istanbul — Santiago, Chile
Beijing — Paris — London — Cairo — Madrid
Milan — Melbourne — Jerusalem — Darfur

11 Chestnut St.
Medford, MA 02155

arrowsmithpress@gmail.com
www.arrowsmithpress.com

The sixty-fifth Arrowsmith book was typeset & designed by
Gerard Robertson for Askold Melnyczuk & Alex Johnson in Garamond
Font

Coming Ashore

New & Selected Poems

Thomas O'Grady

for

Katie

•

Mairéad, Caitríona, Siobhán

•

Cathleen

Jag visste inte vart jag
vände mitt huvud—
med delat synfält
som en häst.

—Tomas Tranströmer

CONTENTS

Part Two: Reckoning

from DELIVERING THE NEWS (2019)

from **WHAT REALLY MATTERS (2000)**

Nuages: New Poems

WHEATFIELD WITH CROWS

Which caught my eye first—that
    feathered burst of black

from the heat-drenched field
    stretched rich as gold

to the road's rough edge . . .
    or the ditch-red fox who,

leaping, snatched it in clenched
    jaws then trotted off?

Part One

Surfacing

COMING ASHORE

after an etching by David Blackwood

We age, and like the rower
in that sea-bobbed dory, his oars

locked in, his broad back arced
like a sail or a bow strung taut

against the task at hand, we chance
an over-the-shoulder glance

at making land that lies ahead;
then turn and face the stern again

where, strain as we might, stroke
after leaden dripping stroke, our former

and forever selves sit tight, their grip
on the gunwales like anchors snagged

in the rippling wake of the past.
How that lad in the prow ignores

the darkening deep—so young,
so sure, so ready to leap ashore.

BOXING DAY

for Caitríona

We walk the strand, collecting stones.
At turning tide, the surf rears up

and shakes its light-flecked mane.
A flight of swans disturbs the sky.

They strain, their mighty wings the thudding
thrum of hoofs pummeling sandy loam—

white stallions galloping neck-and-neck,
three wide, stretching for home.

SPUDS

I promised I'd bring you stones
from the beach, each a perfectly

ovoid form ground down and polished
and buffed by the pounding push

and pull of rising and falling tide,
its unrelenting crash and crush

against the gritty bed of sand.
And I have: a handful of beauties

the size apiece of an infant's fist.
At first, the way they lay in my cap

I thought them like eggs in a nest.
But now as I weigh them one-by-one

then all at once in my palm,
I think of new potatoes,

hard and cool, nuggets from deep
in the red clay at home, freshly dug.

THE CROWS

Cumberland, PEI

They arrive in a rasping riot
to glean the close-cropped

stubble the mowing machine
has left in its billowy wake.

Before the hayrake's simmering
day in the sun, before the baler

drops its twine-tied blocks
of midsummer gold, that scolding

discordant chorus will scour
the meadow down to a nubby

bristle, clear and sheer
as the shimmering gleam

of this morning's breaking
light across the bay, bright

and clean as that rich refrain
we hear in the lane, the pitch-

perfect notes of a solitary
pine-top blackbird's whistle.

ODYSSEUS

Without a trireme's wind-filled sails,
without a rudder, he stood thigh-deep
in a sea-vast field of grain, his long oar

planted upright like a herder's staff.
No winnowing fan at last, its stiff blade
too unwieldy for that feathering task,

it weathered like a man left high and dry
on the open plains, graying then whitening,
flailing against time's rising tide, failing

to separate the wheat from the chaff.

EAST RACE

The sluice gates released,
the East Race unloosed
in a wild whitewater surge,

I stood downstream at midpoint
on the Colfax bridge and felt
the buffeting gush and rush

beneath my feet like the wear
and tear of cascading time,
the froth-topped flow of years.

Far, far from home, the soothing
shoreline come-and-go of tide,
the slow grainy hourglass sift

of salt-tipped sand, I gripped
the balustrade, a pitching prow.
I held to the here and now.

THE RIVER

1. SURFACING

Two cormorants spreading
their dripping wings

to dry. Like musclemen
they stretch and pose

and flex on their soggy
perch, a log lodged

firm against the river's bank.
All preen and sheen,

they give the lie to how
all day they duck

and dive, then surfacing,
paddle, sodden,

breasting the flow, not quite
in over their heads

but fully up to their necks.

2. HERON

The heavens burst. The rain off the river a sudden sideways gush, we ducked and dodged, the glorious day turned hard and gray. We shook our fists at the spilling skies. We cursed our sorry luck. The world awash, we watched a wise old man hunch low on a crooked branch, his sodden collar bunched and frayed, his piercingly yellow eyes aglow.

3. CATCH-AND-RELEASE

All along the river
I stop and talk
with men with rods—

the odd woman, too,
or two—to hear what
they have to say

on weighty matters
like lines and hooks
and bait and bites

or nibbles. A nod,
a shrug, a squint, one eye
always on the flow . . .

Do I disturb their peace?
The words come slow:
large-mouth bass,

catch-and-release . . .
They cast and wait,
draw blanks, then reel

and cast again. I walk
the banks. A salmon leaps.
A blackbird sings.

The evening wakes
in blinking glints and faint
concentric shimmers.

4. SNAPSHOTS

Midges thicken the air.
    Swifts dart and dip in deft
looping swoops. Evening

tips toward dark. A salmon
    leaps, a quicksilver surge
from the river's murky depths.

          •

That lull at dusk. Below
the boathouse a single swan
descends, rowing rowing—
the air a bright river—
the long white scull of itself.

          •

November. The morning
after the first light snow.

A dark shiver. On a river
perch below, a cormorant

buttons his threadbare
coat, tugging at the cuffs,

arranging the collar,
pulling it tight to his throat.

5. DANCE OF THE SEVEN PLATES

The temperature dropped
like a hammer. Snow
began to feather the sky.

We kept an eye on the skin-
thin skims of ice caught up
in the river's flow. They spun

like plates in a Chinese circus.
The cascade spilled downstream
in a shimmering shiver. They took

the plunge. We watched them
dip then tip and slip and fall
in a stunningly silent shatter.

JANUARY

. . . and each day at dawn
a ragged straggle of crows,
a thousand strong, brave
the frosty fog off the river
like wet-suited swimmers
crawling, crawling, crawling
the endless breadth of the sky's
gray channel. Or like weary
soldiers trudging a muddy
retreat through a no man's
land of bottomless murk
and mire . . . Or churchyard
mourners carrying death itself
on their stooped black backs.
Six floors up, eye-level high,
we watch them swarm and swoop
like *Eptesicus fuscus*, a horde
of dive-bombing big brown bats.
We almost cringe and cower.

WEIGHT OF THE WORLD

news photo sequence, Odesa, Ukraine (2022)

The heavy heart of winter,
and from our windowed
perch by the river's edge

we glimpse the steady flow,
the silent shudder and lurch,
of a far-off train on sturdy

trestled tracks eye-high
with the city's low-rise roofs.
Boxcar, gondola, hopper . . .

Freight of the world? A whistle
blows, an engine heaves,
and a world away where roofs

cave in beneath the weight
of war, a man on a platform
turns to brush back tears,

a woman wipes a hazy pane,
a railway carriage judders
and sways . . . then disappears.

THE LAND AGENT

cum spiritu Hiberneuse

On a high horse
even a small man
sits grand as a bishop,

his riding crop a crozier
in his fist, his squat bowler
stiff as a mitre at his brow.

See how the downtrodden
bow before "his grace."
They make him feel so tall.

INFERNO

It sizzled the air all day,
an orange globe of iron tonged
at dawn from the mouth
of a fiery forge and hammered
thin as foil. At dusk it fizzled,
a horseshoe plunged in a blacksmith's
oaken bucket. The western ocean
swallowed it whole. Mist rose
from the meadows like steam.

NUAGES

The uneasiness of words
in these throughother times

on full display—page
upon unseemly scribbled

page, reams of inked-on
paper splayed in disarray

atop the desk—I speak
my mind to a pair of purring

cats and stir my thoughts
while a second cup

of coffee perks and Django
and the Hot Club play.

TURKEY VULTURES

Three red featherless faces
fight and squawk and wait

on a neighbor's roof. A hawk
shadows the sky. The rabbits

and the woodchuck hie
to their boltholes dug beneath

the shed. As we to ours,
a rumrunners' bunkhouse

hidden down a rutted rubble
lane. We huddle in dread.

WAKE-UP CALL

Today, the roads
and all the world around

gone midnight still . . .
meadows, woods and sky

as empty as that posted,
double pole-barred lane

to God-knows-where . . .
I heard, just past high noon,

a rooster crow—three
times—from far away.

FLEDGLINGS

At high noon, their herky-
jerky walk in the meadow
cut short by the shock

of who knows what, a flock
of newly fledged wild turkeys
startled the sky in an upward

burst of clattering wings,
young feathers stiff as quills,
and flew like shards of shrapnel

into springtime's thickening leafage
by the pond. They rattled
the world like clashing sabres.

Life is hard. Theirs and ours.
The air around us shook all day.

HAUTBOIS

Dusk, and from deep
in the deep wood below

an oboe's husky
double-reeded croak

takes breath on the breeze,
one long hollow throat-

blown note. We wait,
ears tuned to the sky.

Darkness falls. Of that
the night heron spoke.

THE MEADOW

1. DAFFODILS

This morning,
spring broke

through the meadow
like egg yolks

dropped in a pan
from on high.

The cold clay
gave way. Color

sizzled and ran.
The brown grass

turned green, the gray
sky suddenly blue.

2. GOLDFINCH

Its dipping wings the dripping
oars of a dory, all flicks

and flitters, it shimmers
the bright-crested tide

of morning, a tipsy boatman
rowing a meadowy sea.

3. LEGS

The deer stood stiff
as a man on stilts

or a runway model
stuck in stiletto heels:

in a buck-bronze thicket
of bamboo shoots

it almost disappeared.

4. SEPTEMBER EQUINOX

The goldfinches are long gone.
This morning, low light stroking

the meadow gray, a hummingbird
flicked at a withering shrub, two

lingering thoughts, and a pair
of catbirds mewed a dissonant song.

Next week leaves will curl and start
to fall, the trees grow spare and dark.

Winds will skirl. Crows will croak,
bluejays caw. The pond beyond

the drystone wall will freeze.
Then, come late March, will thaw.

5. NOVEMBER

Daylight broke
in straight

strafing streaks,
bullet gray,

shredding
the last few

unshed leaves
on the trees

and wiping
the windswept

meadow clean.
The sky wept

buckets of grief,
not rain.

VIBURNUM

Morning on the solstice.
    The summer garden gone
utterly gray with weeds,

we eye the sky, unblinkingly
    blue but for one white wisp,
through a head-high cluster

of glistering ruby beads.

DECEMBER LIGHT

Darkness bookends the day.
Hours unfold like chapters
from dawn to dusk, dog-eared

minutes like pages. We eye
the sky and sniff the air.
Fields reduced to leveled

husks, their harrowed furrows
browed with just a dusting
of snow, we weigh and measure

and count back months and weeks.
We pull our ledgers down
from the shelf. The year reads

in reverse. We ink in blanks
by faint December light.
We tally yield and bounty.

Part Two

Reckoning

INTERNATIONAL HARVESTER McCORMICK No. 5 HAYRAKE

Adamsville, RI

Somehow, country-marrow deep in my soft
city-bred bones, I knew just what to call

that rig, unhitched and ditched as a makeshift
gate for the gap in a steadfast drystone wall.

And somehow knew the workings of that baked-
steel sabre-toothed rack of blades and the yield

left in its tractor-towed wake: rows, neatly raked,
of fresh-mown hay, takings from a well-sown field.

But what do I know now or make of how
it sits in a sorry rut on mud-seized

wheels to fence in like a dying brindled cow
that rusted baler sunk as if to its knees

in a meadow overgrown—long lain fallow—
with weeds and scrubby shrubs and sky-high trees?

THE VISITOR

. . . and then, late one afternoon
in the midst of it all, these hard dark
days, we saw from the kitchen window,
first by the drystone wall in the yard,
then ankle-deep in the pond, an egret
standing tall and bright as a wand.
It glowed, a blinding shaft of light.
When it rose into awkwardly graceful flight,
it took us with it, above the suddenly
budding trees, and beyond.

LONGING

for Mairéad

A room with a view of horses. Who could want more? Two
chestnut fillies, a golden palomino magnificent as light, and
Bailey, that ghostly white mare who one night clip-clopped
down our gravel path like an apparition stepped out of a
book or a dream. This morning in the meadow across the
lane they crowd and nudge the six-barred metal gate as if
longing en masse for another riderless moonlit ride. They
nuzzle each other and nicker. They bother the fence and
wedge their noble heads between the rails. They crunch and
munch the greener grass in reach on the other side.

MORNING GRIND

By breaking dawn, each half-minute
of scattered light leafing another

flittering field guide page of chatter
and song, the stippled sky will fill

to its shimmering brim: bright noise
from heavens above. But I rise still

in the dark, the time of day I love
the most, my soft-soled tread at one

with the earliest stirrings of sound,
a cardinal's whistling whisper,

a flicker's gentle *knock-knock* on wood,
a catbird's mewing call in the sunroom

hedge, and follow the wake-up whiff
of fresh-ground roasted beans to a silent

countertop machine. It all begins
in earnest when I put your favorite cup

in place then listen and watch it work.
It sputters and gurgles and perks.

The kitties add the sweetener underfoot.

MUEZZIN

Hôtel Chellah, Rabat – Morocco

One eye closed, the other staring
straight at a perfect square of light
in the black bathroom door, I lay

awake all night and cursed whatever
it was I ate—that platter of *cous-cous*
shared by many hands, that steaming

tagine at a seedy sidewalk café—
and wished that I could die. And
thought I might . . . until I drifted

in a fevered state and replayed,
dreaming, that scene in the *souk*:
a feral *qitt*, its pleading eyes

white weeping sores, its coat a filthy
infested mess. Did I scratch its tattered
ears and stroke its back, its matted head,

and wonder had it even one life left?
At dawn I heard the *muezzin* call.
I stirred. Then stretched and yawned.

Then rose as if from the dead.

LISTENING TO JOSEF LOCKE

Clara, Co. Offaly

Count Your Blessings, he sang, and *Hear My Song*,
the pitched range and reach of his rich tenor voice
a summons so mellifluously strong
that we did both. As if we had a choice . . .
As if like tune-deaf cynics we could resist
the pure allure of lyric sentiment,
the worsted woolen weave of midland mist
so thick that even *Come Back to Sorrento*
rings like a sea-washed siren's seductive thrall—
The Isle of Innisfree . . . *I'll Take You Home* . . .
how sweet-toned bog-soft airs become the call
to land a Pan Am pilot in this poem.
In a sleek red roadster—roof down!—he swept
into town. His father's sister stared, then wept.

HERMITAGE

after the Irish of
Bro. S. Ó Maoile

I. CELIBACY

Night falls, an iron
doorlatch dark

and tight. I stand
by the window

and watch. Gray, gray
with green envy,

I hear the river
froth and flow.

II. SACRAMENT

The rushlight trembles.
My hands shake.

A jug shimmers
on a high shelf.

I shudder. Then bow
my head and pour.

Devout acolyte
to myself.

III. SILENCE

Touch-and-go of teeth
and tongue, I mouth

my name through
blistering lips.

I hunger to speak,
but eat my words.

My whisper drowns
in thirsty sips.

IV. LAUDATE

The river sighs.
I stretch. I rise.

A heron croaks
to wake the day.

A cormorant strikes
its wingspread pose.

I kneel. I raise
my arms. I pray.

DIZZYING

That night we heard him take flight in the conference room of a downtown South Bend hotel, trumpet bell bent up toward the stars, a gleaming exotic bloom, we held our breath, his highwire acrobatic notes scaling the rolled-back partition walls like searching beams of light, pouched cheeks pushing and pitching those flaring flurries beyond the soundproofed drop-ceiling tiles. How he climbed and climbed those ladder rungs of ledger lines inside his head, a death-defying flying trapeze of arpeggiated style, until . . . Did he make his Irish exit through the roof? The band played on and on. We were young in the spring of '84. We waited and waited, expecting more.

6 x 6

1. CHARLIE CHRISTIAN

Last night, listening once again to *Solo Flight*,
to note after single-string note strung in long strands
through chorus after mightily cadenced chorus
(Benny Goodman and his Orchestra in full swing) . . .
the thought of bows knotted on a kite's trailing tail,
of genius dying young, of *Gone With "What" Wind*.

2. DJANGO REINHARDT

A nightmare cry—*Au feu! Au feu!*—in a gypsy's
rolling house of dreams (*Manoir de mes Rêves*) come true.
Then the scream of splintering back, neck, pearl-flecked
    fretboard
(cured kindling, fuel for the pyre), the whip-stroke spring
of snapped steel, and fingers fused—*mon Dieu!* . . . how he
    played
with fire—into trembling curls like wisps of white smoke.

3. LES PAUL

Is this what Edison meant ("To invent, you need
a good imagination and a pile of junk") . . .
or dreamt—an improvised tangle of tubes and wires,
a hardwood hunk (railroad steel dense), "inspiration"
one percent, "perspiration" the rest? Mere prelude
to a fugue: "chained lightning" unloosed in *Subterfuge*.

4. BARNEY KESSEL

Somehow, picking impeccable runs and deftly
stitched chords from the seemingly seamless warp and weft
of worn standards—*My Old Flame, Embraceable You*—
the right hand understands what the left one will do . . .
Picture spiffed-up partners gracing a spotlit floor.
Now "look" at this: that rug-cutting riff of *Let's Cook!*

5. GRANT GREEN

Try transcribing even a single dexterous line
of Hank Mobley's *Workout* . . . or *Smokin'* (that session
from '61) and watch the inked nib flick, nimbly,
glistening beads, quicksilver slick, across the staves.
Precious gemstones? (Emeralds? Polished peas of jade?)
Translucent black pearls . . . their sheen every shade of green.

6. WES MONTGOMERY

Twisted Blues, West Coast Blues, Born to Be Blue . . . And yet
those pulse-strong double-stopped strokes of pure callused
    pluck,
his trademark thumb-strummed octaves, calling out rhyming,
chiming overtones like a steepled, rope-hung bell
swung with bronze-bright appeal. That clapping tongue—the
    gong,
the hum—in *Naptown Blues* . . . no dark summoning knell.

THIS IS MY STORY, THIS IS MY SONG

Well, You Needn't, I hummed—
    the first two bars. Then *Ruby,*
        My Dear—a whole half-chorus.
            Epistrophy next, a riff of staggered

steps, connect-the-dotted lines
    of notes deranged in space
        like see-through walls of a house
            built just off-plumb. What Monk's

benighted Nellie knew? *Straight,*
    No Chaser her tangled double-helix
        keyboard theme, she spent her days
            pent up by dissonant angles—

mirrors, photos, artwork badly hung—
    until Thelonious, full of tricks,
        half-madly hammered out a scheme
            to nail the crooked clock-face

in its place. Had he not heard dark
    spirits lurk where no light falls?
        Small wonder *Brilliant Corners*
            fills my brain: time transfixed,

our Brazilian cleaners come and gone,
    Carmen and her crew, I wander room
        to spotless room resetting frames
            their *Misterioso* notions left askew.

THE REAL BOOK

Isn't It Romantic?
Just You, Just Me
When Lights Are Low

All of Me
All of You
Embraceable You
My One and Only Love

All the Things You Are
My Old Flame
Satin Doll
Stella By Starlight
Angel Eyes
My Funny Valentine
Come Rain or Come Shine

My Romance
My Little Suede Shoes
Little Rootie Tootie
The Girl from Ipanema
Mercy, Mercy, Mercy
In Case You Haven't Heard
I Got It Bad

Don't Blame Me
The Nearness of You
The Way You Look Tonight
Mellow Mood
Stardust
Old Devil Moon

Fly Me to the Moon

Well You Needn't
It Don't Mean a Thing
How Insensitive
Out of Nowhere
Careless Love
Fools Rush In

It Could Happen to You

Ask Me Now
'Round Midnight
Now's the Time
Speak Low
Softly, as in a Morning Sunrise
How High the Moon

Groovin' High

THE RECKONING

A shrug, a long once-over, twice, from nape
to crown, a drawn-out stretching yawn, a frown:

that day I begged my barber, Barbara Ann,
to trim a gray-maned decade from my life—

to please the wife, I hastened to explain,
who swore last night she wed a younger man.

Then *Sit* her fingers snapped and tapped the throne
and draped me in a cape from throat to lap.

Then comb and buzzing clippers, razor, shears . . .
a stepping back and forth . . . a tuneless hum . . .

a shaggy carpet spreading thick as years—
the feathery fall of silver-templed time!

The brush-off next, a mint-tipped sigh: "I tried."
The glinting mirror brought us eye to eye.

AT THE ALBERTINA, VIENNA

They flow, one into another, like old
city squares, each gallery wall of frames

a leaning rowhouse block of gleaming street-
level windows, heavy curtains drawn back

as if to let alluring eyes gaze out:
Kirchner's *Dodo* and *Two Nudes in a Room* . . .

Picasso's bevy of bosomy belles . . .
Mueller's *Bathing Girls at the Forest Pond* . . .

•

Exotic and erotic: Manguin . . . Matisse . . .
Modigliani's *Young Woman in a Shirt* . . .

Was it hard to skirt past their beguiling stares?
Heckel . . . Vallotton . . . I toed the viewer's line

until *Nu Gris de Profil* by Bonnard.
That so familiar form: his wife or mine?

DIE MÄDCHEN MEINER TRÄUME

after Kirchner

Forgive me, love: that stylish broad-brimmed hat
may be the topper—Parisian *haute couture*—

but how could I (improper as it seems)
not stop and stare when there she stood in flesh

and blood and light of day, just so picture
perfect, a figure fit for a boudoir wall . . .

and yes (I must admit), *the girl of my dreams* . . .
with all her precious goods on rare display?

I know you know I swore (in heart and head)
to sip no crimson lips but yours . . . but oh—

the promise that those ruby slippers spoke:
Mein Herr, you're not in Kansas anymore.

And yet, *bei Gott* (I do declare): *had she
been you instead* . . . And then, *mein Schatz*, I woke.

VARIATIONS ON A THEME

1. MYTHOS

We are mortal. We all must fall.
Even the hero's Hephaestian
shield could not forestall forever
the flint-tipped bolt and jolt of fate.
Fault his mother that her dipping grip
proved lethal as any armor's breach?
The great gods have their own designs.
Take heed, dear reader: to each of us
an Achilles heel has been assigned.
But take heart too: I married mine.

2. WHAT SAW THE GODS . . .

What saw the gods last night as we drifted
in that acrobatic twist and tangle,
your fingers a tender cuff on my wrist,
your ankle in the clasping grasp of my hand—
our limbs the weathered ribs, the splintered keel
and mast of a half-buried shipwreck splayed
across an uncharted desolate strand?

•

Or did they, as mere mortals do, connect
those dots and spell out in the stars' array
a tale of castaway survivors pitched
and tossed in a tiny tideswept dory . . .
that old sort of story, the stuff of myth—
lost lovers holding on for dear life, at sea
forever in constellated glory?

3. BOXCARS

Everywhere, it seems, in the middle
of nowhere—these midwestern plains
that spread in all directions like a good
long life lived out but not done yet—
they sit, in my mind always in twos,

on sidetracks buried in autumnal stubble
and husks, slowed to a stop but, stubbornly,
even slower to rust to dust, their sliding
doors slid wide to frame the world
just as far as the mortal eye can see.

•

And farther still to a café à Paris—
Au Chien Qui Fume—where once
I watched, from across the room,
another knuckly coupling, a gnarly
knot of fingers . . . swollen, arthritic,

thick as thumbs . . . coming to tabletop
grips while coffees cooled and rain rose
as steam from sodden layers of matted wool.
Hands locked in tandem, the present holding
to the past. How hard to make love last?

UAIGNEAS

1. AUGUST

The sun rose red as rust.

I stood and watched and waved
as you chugged up the narrow
tracks of the loose clay lane,

brake lights blinking farewell
in your wake . . . lanterns swung
from a swaying caboose.

Summer followed in huffing
steam engine puffs of dust.

2. PHILOSOPHY

Absence is presence,
or so the wise men teach,

my head deducing a grim
phantom limb. That said,

tonight our days apart
yawn wide as a slough

of despond: the existential
void. I reach across

your side of the bed;
the emptiness swallows

my unschooled heart.

3. IARMHAIREACHT*

To dream is to drown.
I wake each day

in a deep blue pool,
the waters of sleep.

The coffee makes.
You rise from the depths,

dawn's blooming bouquet.
I catch my breath.

** the loneliness you feel at cockcrow, when you are
the only person awake and experience that existential
pang of disconnection, of not belonging*

ARS POETICA

Springtime, and the neighbors'
ventriloquial quail trebles

from his backyard hutch
rich throat-thrown quavers,

shrill trills pitched over fences
and hedges, troubled tones

projected high and hard
through quivering double-glazed

panes of glass and shuddering
shingled walls. How the frail

air shivers at his hermitic art,
note after far-flung trembling

note, an aching mating call
sung out from heart to heart.

CARDIGAN DAYS, 1964

Epithalamion for Siobhán & Tim

Some learn their science the hard way,
even Newton's spelled-out law of motion:
Momentum = *Mass* x *Speed* . . .

Take that fleet of makeshift flatbeds—
two-by-fours and sheets of grainy
plywood, wobbly wire-spoked wheels

from a baby sister's pram, a frayed
hank of clothesline rope held pulley-
taut like a sulkied trotter's reins.

How those school's-out schoolboys
put physics to the test—. . . *unless*
obstructed by an outside force—

and failed when halfway down
the steep-pitched course they hit
the not-so-level level-crossing tracks

with a train-wreck choral shout
of sky-borne flailing bodies,
snapping axles, splintering boards,

snipped cotter pins, and sun-struck
spinning rims. Except for one:
my cousin in a perfect marriage

of function and form—a welded,
bolted crate-like cart with tiller
steering . . . and pneumatic tires.

How he rode on air and passed
the rest with flying bunting colors . . .
and won by a country mile!

Let them cry foul. All's fair when push
comes to shove in a soapbox derby.
All's fair, my dears, in love.

from Delivering the News

(2019)

CONTROLLED BURN

The world had spun, the days grown longer,
brighter, endless winter's dusk-gray snowpack
melted into muddy piles of salt and sand

and gravelly silt, glinting grit. The windows
open wide, the globe a-tilt on the deep-set sill,
we slouched at our high school desks and watched

a rumble of red and ringing gold pull up
and firemen descend from the shining pumper
like a swarm of ravening crows full bent

on scouring a close-cropped autumn field.
But this was spring and that field no spreading meadow
of fresh-mown hay but an unkempt urban plot

of tussocky hummocks matted into mangy tufts,
the scraggly fur of an old dog's corpse, ripe
with decay and rot until brought near boiling

by a week of the lengthening sun's low simmer.
And so to stave off random sparks—the flick
of some stray match or a truant's tossed butt—

the captain touched a torch to the tangled mass
and set that clumpy lot ablaze . . . though not
to let it burn until burnt out of its own accord.

Does nature daydream summer? Minds bored numb
by the dusty white noise squeak of chalk,
the teacher, heedless, yammering on and on,

we sat, the whole room, rapt by the spectacle below
of a shimmering brigade fanned out across that bleak
half-acre: flames licking like crested waves

at knee-high boots, they waded to their ankles
armed not with coiling hoses but with brooms—
stunted Curling Club castoffs, bristles bound tight

as glowing sheaves of Saskatchewan wheat—to beat
that conflagration down to smoldering earth.
We had learned already what happens next:

a night or two of drenching rain and, by the book,
a scorched wasteland sprouts green shoots of life.
The turning world will spawn its own rebirth.

DELIVERING THE NEWS

On wild March days that cotton canvas sack
held rain like a tent and hung so low it thumped

a sodden beat like a leaden weapon sheathed
against my thigh. Schoolboy short, I cinched the strap

up high in a knuckled knot (my collarbone
still sports a phantom bruise) and shouldered on.

From door to door I bore the soggy news,
street by street—Churchill Avenue, Spring Park Road . . .

•

War, Pestilence, Famine, Death. Was I deaf
to the headline roar of my unwieldy load?

Weight of the world. Art of the backhand toss.
The guileless messenger shot at and missed.

On Friday nights I tallied my receipts
and somehow ended, always, at a loss.

STEERS

Today I walked the shore road
past a field of steers. Swaggering

block-shouldered anvil-browed brutes,
taut muscle and gristle, sheer beef

to the heels . . . they gave me the eye.
Do heavy-breathing beasts see red

en masse? I returned the stare
through sagging barbed-wire strands

until in phantom fear my knees
went weak and my heart skipped

decades back to that hard lesson
learned in high school hallways—

the bruising jostle and jam
of elbow jabs and hip checks,

slew-foot trip-ups, locker slams . . .
all life's indignities rehearsed

before the morning bell's
first call. Mere oxen in the sun?

Meekly, I inhaled salt air.
Even a gelded bull has horns.

TWIST

The spitshine on my winedark
wingtip brogues a sunburst splash,
a burnished chestnut sheen,

I blink back fifty autumns
to a croaking high noon summons
from a rickety porch, a tarnished

nickel clutched in a knuckly fist:
how that scaresome crone,
her gummy drooling grin

a crooked picket fence
of licorice nibs, stopped me short
in my trudging schoolboy tracks.

How I turned heel and ran,
both ways, to fill her cornerstore
request. How my palm reeked

for days from that scissored snip,
a cud cut from a seeping braid
of tar, wax paper-wrapped:

a gob, molasses-soft, of cured
tobacco . . . a pruned "fig"
of Hickey & Nicholson twist.

THREE COWS

The morning my brother laid
a rueful hand on that curvaceous
haunch—the sloped fender

of his rumble-seated Dodge
(cash on demand, *finis*)—
my mother saw in that tender

touch, his sad *adieu* to an antique
coupe, her father's kindly thump
(his heavy heart) on their cow's

wide rump, drooping dugs
dried up, as she swayed behind
the tanner's tumbrel cart.

So it happens, time's hard
stroke dealt and felt. My turn
today to slap a broad backside,

a no-longer-limber hip.
Our Springer's pelt a lumbering
Holstein heifer's paint-patch hide,

she looked, a newly weaned pup,
a half-pint calf. We dubbed her,
a dog's life ago, *La vache.*

COLD SHOULDER

Nights when my wife complains of "the cold shoulder,"
shrugging and tugging for, she says, her fair share
of the covers, hanging on for dear life
to the precipitous edge of the bed—
her half halved again—I ask have I told her
of the time I walked three miles in a threadbare
coat . . . thirty below and the wind like a knife,
my ears almost cut from my hatless head.

Of how I then thawed out each frostbitten part—
mittenless fingers, the tip of my nose—
in the plush-deep warmth of a feline side.
Might this melt even a blanketless heart?
How now another cat, grown chill as the snows,
stakes in old age a claim on the great divide.

BLAST

It hit so close, that lightning bolt
I dodged last summer, its fiery flash
and jag-toothed crash a muzzleloader's
loud-mouthed shout. I thought
I had been shot.
                    But not shot
through and through, struck
to the core, like that old windbreak
birch, a marker for our measured
plot of land. Before it went, it stood,
withstood, for years, beset by blast,
a canker, or a cancer, aimed at trees . . .
insidious disease. I dodged that too,
the doctor said, his tight-lipped talk
a jolt from the blue.
                        "A near miss,"
and yet, like voltage heaven-sent,
it cleared the air and cleared the view.
Let thunder roar. Stunned sunlight pours
on our weed-wild field, floods
gently sloped meadows, drains
down to the whispering shore.

ALCHEMY

Just our luck. Morning
unloads rain in buckets,
leaden gray. We watch

the sky and wait. We muck
about and pace and place
the day on hold. By noon

we write it off and sigh.
Hours pass. We scoff
at forecasts painted blue.

O ye of little faith! A bold
crow barks a brazen note
of hope behind the barns.

The clouds begin to yield
and lift, pale rays leak through.
Then evening sun erupts.

We walk the lane. Life brightens.
Flooding light weaves braided gold
from a field of sodden grain.

HERMIT CRABS

By noon tomorrow,
    all here receding glance
by rearview glance

at endlessly fading gray,
    mile after multiplying mile,
I'll picture how today—right now,

the tide at lowest ebb,
    the brick-red bars of sand
holding mirrors to the cloudless sky—

my plodding tread perturbed
    in a rippling pool a scurry
of legs, a disembodied

creature carrying home
    upon its back.
I carry mine in my head.

SEEING RED

Blizzard-bound, snowed
under, walled-in . . . swallowed
by a whirling world

of white, a mapless maze
of shifting waist-deep drifts,
he wades and wallows.

His hedgerows bent—
though not like ours,
beneath the weight of war

and sorrow . . . once more
the winter of our discontent—
he looks ahead as if

to greener pastures.
Hapless cattle lowing
to be fed, he holds his course,

led—as we are too—
by the heartening blaze
of red that frames the doors,

the eaves, the corner trim
of every outlying
Island barn and shed.

ENVOI

Half-past dawn. Croaked awake, we watch the sky
wake too, lead-gray, with the slow lurching launch
of a half-dozen origami cranes—
great blue herons—unfolding from their swaying

pine-top perch above our ruddy rutted lane.
They breast the air, a fleet of tattered flags
unfurling stroke by rowing stroke against
the wave-cresting wind . . . The morning hours pass.

Noontime comes and goes. The tide ebbs and flows.
We eye the glass-bright bay for fabric hung
on creaking frames of ribs and spine—the flight
of tail-trailing kites let loose and blown astray.

·

Our hearts rise with the sinking sun. Dusk falls.
At end of day, we all come home to roost.

SAILING FROM AN ISLAND

What more could we lose chancing one last glance
at the gray-toned sheet unwinding behind
us where every hill and straight-drilled field slants

to the shore? Look: the whole world seems inclined
to salt at this dim hour—the windbreak pines
along the lanes, sluggish cattle reclined

in huddled herds, rolled haybales stored in lines
against dark barns, all reduced to hazy
shades and forms. See how pre-dawn light refines

away the vibrant reds and greens—that crazy
quilt of midday color stretched end to end
on this sea-hemmed place. Not for the lazy

or hard-of-rising, or those who would spend
an extra half-morning *at home*, this road
where dipping headlamps redefine each bend

will rise to meet all honoring the code
of catching the day's first boat—bred to gauge
setting out (custom's momentum unslowed

by year upon year of added baggage)
from measureless, meaningless miles away.
Who would forego this true rite of passage—

this rush and race against time's steady sway?

THE RISING

I rose to watch the morning rise
from the dark sloping bay of meadow,
the dark woods below, the dark hills beyond.

Slowly . . . *slowly* daybreak's great blue heron
shifted stiffly on its stilted legs. My coffee
sat unstirred, the black pool of night.

I sipped. I sipped again.
I stepped into stillness.
Light lifted into gray creaking flight.

CORTONA

The road a comma,
a curving double-clutching
climb to a round plateau,

we paused right there—
halfway to the hill town's
cobbled square—and caught

our breath at the daybreak view
from terracotta rooftop
height. Were we walking

on air? A pure panorama
that sparkling plain below!
Look down, I thought,

and see like mighty gods
the wide world still at rest.
Or else like mere mortals:

looked down upon and blessed.

AT McNELLO'S

Inniskeen, Co. Monaghan

Hard men. Punters. A thirst for the ponies.
I nursed my pint in the shadows and watched

their equine faces rise then fall as they watched
the Newmarket card play out, race by race,

and, true to form, maligned an afternoon
misspent on a slate of boldly misplaced

wagers: It's My Time, Slip Sliding Away,
Sovereign Debt . . . top tips turned to also-rans.

·

Hope. The longshot we ride blinkered every day.
Just ask that loveblind lad behind the bar.

Run ragged, pillar to post, he liked his odds
phoning bets to the bookie's coy daughter.

"A good-looking voice." He rang up again.
"Tell us her name, boys." She had him haltered.

AN SLATÓIR

Avondale, PEI

Harvest time. The high blue skies of August. The land aglow
with gold. His brothers grown into two tall oaks, straight and
true, the third son slouched in their shadow thrown along
the field's red edge. Would this be the year? The old man
coughed, his body bent like a bleach-dyed windbreak pine. He
pointed. "You and you," he said. One brother took his seat in
the jiggling rig, the other took the mare's compliant blinkered
head. "And you . . ." He knew that nod. He knew his lot. He
took up his rod. His lowly job to hold erect the grain before
the mower.

SMOKE SIGNALS

We shoulder what we can.
The morning sky's red clouds
a warning—*each day aim true*—

I sat astride my two-wheeled steed
and plucked with my mind
the high-strung bow of love.

I knew the trail led home.
What message would I code
that you could read . . .

and how deliver? My hands
in the grip of braking, steering . . .
I slung across my back

three long-stemmed roses, cellophane-
wrapped. My heart was aquiver.

THE ODYSSEY

Athena, I thought: the gray-eyed goddess
(musing behind her back) . . . dressing to kill—
girding skirted loins for a boardroom war—
so that when the mirror said "Make the bed,"
I dreamt my drowsing self Odysseus
endowed with a journeyman joiner's skill,
crafting from an olive trunk shafting the floor
a cornerpost doweled for a marriage stead.

Complacencies of a rumpled duvet . . .
of unplumped pillows . . . of hand-loomed cotton sheets
(a trireme's billowing sails!) thread-count rich.
Did Olympus frown on Penelope,
or deem undone deeds stay-at-homer feats?
Faithful—boudoir-bound—I wait without a stitch.

PICASSO

"You flatter us either way," she laughs—
    my winsome wife—when, eyeing
        her felicitous form, those alluring
            curves arranged in languidly

mattressed lines of limbs and torso
    defined as if carved out by the razor-
        thin tip of some great creator's
            scimitar-bladed knife,

I pause in mid-arpeggio—O
    the shameless appeal of shapely
        chords . . . *Misty, Body and Soul,*
            My Foolish Heart—

and, picturing Picasso's linocut
    Woman Reclining and Picador
        Playing Guitar, ask: "Which
            holds up the mirror—art or life?"

DOUBLING ON BRASS

Later, we'll sweep our rosined bows
across the singing strings and saw out
to the concert-master's measured

baton beat the overture's sweet
curtain-raising strains, the cascading rush
of notes arranged to hush the restless

to the edge of their seats. We'll watch
from our orchestral perch the tent flaps close,
the world reduced to a single shining ring.

•

But now we're cued to the drum major's
silver-crowned mace and locked in marching step
with the leggy stride of the top-hatted man on stilts,

the twirlers' swirling pace, the zoo of jungle cats
caged-in on horse-drawn carts, the slow stampede
of pachyderms on parade. Even our hearts race

at the snare's bright roll. We are the trombone's
slippery slide, the trumpet's golden blare.
The tuba's *oom-pah-oom-pah* brings up the rear.

from What Really Matters
(2000)

DARK HORSES

Steady to the end,
the limits of his life
defined by fences, hedges,

headlands in a field,
he chose a day of rest
as if he knew the work

could wait, then sought
final comfort circling
square familiar corners,

sniffing for his brother
dark horse death. We
should pray for such grace,

that bred-in-the-bone
knowing what we're called to,
early on: plowing, poeming,

harvesting the sea. Would
that bareback rider raking
Irish moss at Skinner's Pond

agree? In my dream he clutches
madly at a white-flecked mane.
I wake when the anvil ocean bed

leaps up to meet the surging
sledge of beast and tide.

BLOODLINES

I

Remember how we'd hike off every spring,
mother-bundled brothers striking outbound
streets like born-and-bred hobos just dying
to run away from home? Now we astound
our wide-flung selves to admit that once mere
names—Elm Avenue, Malpeque Road—could work
their exotic charm as far as Belvedere
and the last leg-wearying uphill trek
before the College bleachers. Then the race
to see who'd reach the railway platform first!
There, braced by a brownbag lunch, we'd all face
east, each year excited enough to burst.
Never, though, did our track-tuned ears detect
an oncoming train. What did we expect?

II

What should we have expected, standing there
at a whistlestop siding? Did we think
that just around the bend—the fixed point where
the familiar vanishes in a blink—
destiny could lie? If only native
wisdom had swung its lantern's guiding light
on that illusion—lent true perspective
to our final destination! We might
have been content to spend predictable
patient lives, as at home as the railroad
agent's wife who set meals on the table
timed to the minute the station clock showed.
Our grandfather wisely mastered the urge
to wander where parallel lines converge.

CORMORANTS

So. The cormorants have come home
to roost. Crook-necked upright bats,
I thought at first: Pictou Landing,
twenty years ago. Bagpipes balanced
on cabers. Unlikely twisted birds.

Now whole colonies host wherever
web-clawed perch, or purchase,
might be had: a half-sunken pier
at St. Catherine's, the pilings
of long-gone Hillsborough Bridge.

Misshapen blow-ins from over
the Strait. Brine-blackened sticks.
Why would I envy your more-than-
native wingspread ease? Wind-
whipped remnants of tarpaper shacks.

EXILE

Sometimes, exile makes the heart
grow harder than the iron edge,
exposed at last, of a long-discarded
cartwheel in the sand. The calloused
sole of absence, distance dulls
all but the phantom pain of taking
leave until I walk this stony
foreign shore.

At home the russet strand gives way
beneath soft feet except
where knuckly knots of mussels
barnacle themselves to salt-brushed
shelves of shale. Encrusted
so, not hardened to the core,
I suffer once more that surging bone-
deep hurt of parting. *At home . . .*
Washed by that tide, my brittle bedrock
heart erodes.

CATTLE CROSSING AT ARGYLE SHORE

I

So distraught I felt, for days afterward,
at the thought of our having gotten caught
in a scene straight from a 10¢ postcard—
Cattle Crossing at Argyle Shore. We bought
into it so gratefully—that vignette
of man and beast, a tableau vivant staged
as if to show how time's rough tide had yet
to mark the spirit of that place. Assuaged
by the pastoral—*genius loci* at large—
we savored with such bona fide pleasure
how an incidental turning (the urge
of *here!* or *there!*) allowed us to measure
an archetypal moment like purists
of "the Island way of life." Or tourists.

II

Tourists. Visitors. Company from away.
Fresh off the ferry from "the Boston states."
(So quickly wide-eyed wonder can betray—
as surely as accents or license plates.)
Outsiders. Blow-ins. Mere seasonal strays.
Who, truly native-born, could be romanced
as easily as that? *Rarae aves*
we seemed indeed (strange breed) until I chanced
upon nature's fact that the two-dozen
brown-headed cowbirds we counted that day
were hatched and reared in foster nests—that when
fully fledged they made their unerring way
back to the cattle-stalking flock: to *home*.
Really we had gotten caught in a poem.

THANKSGIVING

Summers we'd give thanks to be city born
and bred when, come mid-August, our country
cousins trudged two weeks ahead to the stern
task of learning, the clean-cut drudgery
of school. Of course, in October we'd curse
the luck that gave them a fortnight repeal
of break-knuckle rules—though what could be worse
than digging potatoes in muck-caked fields?
Who, in their right minds, would envy that chore,
and pray—in late November, a thousand
miles and many years away—to restore
themselves by the grace of clay-coated hands?
Elbow-deep in a sack of unscrubbed spuds,
we swear never to wash off that red mud.

TRANSMIGRATION

Each year, predictably
    as birds, or seasons—
        sometimes early,
           sometimes late—

we return to find the scene
    along our half-mile
        stretch of Island shore
          exactly

as we held it in our minds,
    its soul intact.
        If only our souls too
          could always feel

as whole as then, as
    thoroughly at home as when,
        surrounded by
          a quarrelsome choir

of gulls and raucous crows—
    the world's discordant chorus—
        a half-dozen
          great blue herons

strike their so serenely
    steady pose. How we envy
        such unstudied grace—
          their stock-still grip

in tidal pools and eddies,
    the undistracted gaze of
        creatures designed to bear
           precisely

the burden of their own calm
    waiting. What must we do
        to have our souls' weight
           lifted so, to make

the half-composed complete?
    What might dull the clamor
        of this crow-and-gull life?
           Last week,

on a mid-December morning,
    dying for home, we saw
        a solitary heron
           in full flight.

AUGURIES

No more playing blind,
casting about
as if miscast in myth,

seeking
in the feathered beat
of birds some sign:

today, ears cupped
to the August sky, we
eyed with awe

the northern harrier's
scouring scowl across
a fresh-mown meadow.

How the domestic
turns exotic
in a time of change—

the heron's croaking
homeward thrust;
the kingfisher's breakneck

plunge in a crested bay;
the osprey's taloned
plummet a sun-flung blade!

Once again,
midsummer's swooping loops
of swallows reduced,

resigned to lining wires
along the boat-bound
lane,

our last week
reads like a field guide
to the art of flight.

A POEM LEAVES NO MORE MARK

A poem leaves no more mark
upon the world than a gull's

dull cry at noon; or a gust
across the bay. Or the Point Prim

beacon blinking in a late-home
trawler's wake. What have I

to show for finding quiet
harbor here? Angel wings spread

on rippled bars, my daughters
singing *Echo!* off the cliffs:

a prayer makes time stand still.
A poem leaves no more mark

than whirlpools spooling thimbles
into rock at turning tide:

a fingerhold (and no more)
on a solid sandstone shore.

VALEDICTION

I

The sea is not so calm
tonight.

This morning, as the tide
edged high against that bouldered
bluff that points a narrow channel
through the strait, we watched
a pair of herring gulls sit fat
as fallen skaters on a pond—
so sheer the surface lay.

Across the bay the island, too,
seemed more to hover than to float,
as if by breaking light a hand-shaped
cloud had brushed a tromp l'oeil
mural at the pearl-gray seam
of crestless swells and ray-
refracting sky. O how I wished
for the same deft touch to sketch
that scene inside an opalescent
shell: a fresco limned in miniature—
in shimmering aquarelle.

II

By noon, though, when at lowest
ebb the basin had drained to turbid
pools and shoals of mud-caked mussels
black as clotted ink, we noticed
most the ring of briny wrack left
cluttering our shore. More subtly
than that shifting archipelago
of terns we almost missed until
like wind-churned spray they lifted
and dispersed, the morning scape
had changed as if a scalpel-wielding
fist had scraped a luminescent
wash to yield—belied by palimpsest—
much starker tones of grief.

O for belief in auguries:
to see at dusk on our final night
that great blue heron homing—silent,
sure, a lambent form in numinous
relief against descending dark—
we might have deemed our own
departure true to natural design.
Instead, eyes shut, we listen
to the white-capped slap and slop
of rising surf upon the sharp-faced
scarp that lines our cove. How
could we, following portents, feel
resigned to setting out? Tomorrow
when dawn falters through an iridescent
mist, those cliffs—like ruddy cheeks—
will be streaked with salt.

REDEMPTION

To think that all that time we blamed the spite
of our neighbors—a rabid, demented
pack of God-forsaken, fiend-tormented
curs (though more bark behind our backs than bite)—
on that dismembered Christ, *sans* crucifix,
I unearthed in the garden our first month there,
piercing its heart with the rake's cruel spear:
one of my weekend centurion's tricks.

Jesus wept! If only we had known how
jackals sense calamity in the air—
hovering pestilence, flood, famine, drought:
our fault to have overlooked that horseshoe
hanging wrongside up I found our seventh year.
We left before our luck had all run out.

PAGANINI

Capriccioso. Capricious as the devil,
if half the tales his devotees tell

ring with even a crooked crotchet
of gospel truth. My favorite

one of all makes Nero turn over
with envy in his grave (wherever

that high-strung fiddler, immodest
to the end—*What an artist*

the world is losing in me!—
may lie): the time in London he

taught an entire orchestra
how to play with fire. *Scordatura.*

Pizzicato. Trills. Harmonics.
Multiple stopping. All the tricks

in the book! And every demi-
semiquaver so dazzlingly

right on cue that no awestruck,
dumbfounded blameless mortal took

note of how minor parts succumb
to a guttering music-desk flame.

Give old Niccolò his due:
for such a gift, by God, I too

would sell my soul at any price.
Il Maestro's forte—no caprice—

like a candle burns just once.
Call it *sprezzatura*: nonchalance.

THE TEST OF THE BOW

Remembering Michael Coleman

Before he faced the suitors in the hall,
he proved himself by plucking high-strung gut
until it hummed a single note. So pure
it sang—a ringing, feathered bolt of sound—
that even brazen bucks (their noisy brawl
an antidote for doubt) fell still; around
the walls skirts quivered for the first strong cut,
the larksome thrill of severed air.
                                        So sure,
then, one man stood above this throng, elbow
arced, fingers poised to throw them into thrall.
What goddess nodded portent from the door?
He bowed toward his muse, that blood should flow:
brash bodies moved, then shoved to fill the floor.
He proved himself the master of them all.

AFTER LOOKING INTO R. J. O'DUFFY'S *HISTORIC GRAVES IN GLASNEVIN CEMETERY* (1915)

—Let us go round by the chief's grave, Hynes said. We have time.

I

We had time that day, Dublin's high noon sun
conspiring at every turn to recast

classic forms, to play like mutating shadows
on the winding sheets of tarmacadam,

gravel, dirt: my Aeneas to your Virgil
to my Dante—back and forth in the land

of the dead. Father and son, we took heart
against the heat at Parnell's ivy-bordered

bower, almost marveling that no guardian
strained to roll away the stone, the quarried

mass a praying people laid out to atone
for mortal guilt: the weight of a great man gone.

II

Gone but not forgotten, we left unsaid,
not daring to name the specter of our own

dark end: with what utter finality
ordinary lives recede. Today, a book

returned me to that sweltering hour spent
searching through the patternless warp and weft

of paths for a spot we called *the weaver's grave*,
a short-lived writer's plot—to how we shivered

there, worn viators, in the sheer candescence
shimmering off the bleached unseeded clay:

how our stunted shadows seemed to unravel
to bleary shades of gray, then disappear.

A PRAYER FOR MY DAUGHTERS

Outside another storm is howling; more
terrific than the one a poet heard
so many years ago, this tempest's roar
has loosened like a pickaxe the mortared
brick of faith. No master mason, I shore
up with doubtful timber—knotty, tortured
slabs of dim thought—the burden-bearing wall
of overwrought belief. It may yet fall.

On nights like this I shudder when, resigned
to fitful rest (at best), I rise to gaze
upon seraphic forms. Sprawled in purblind
bliss—so seemingly immune to my malaise—
those shadowy innocents call to mind
pale plastercast cherubs psaltering praise
from vaulted heights: rapture in high relief,
keystone rosettes in overarching grief.

Faultless harbingers of redeeming grace,
or heralds of the firmament's collapse?
Against the dark, my smarting eyes retrace
an archived image of nave, transept, apse—
a cathedral's heart—ravaged by the race
of wildfire over oak and stone. Perhaps
the answer lies buried in smoke-stained panes,
a sharded puzzle in rubbled remains.

Faith of my father, assuage my despair!
(Once, he saw in the glinting gilt-framed glass
on a print—*The Holy Family*, I swear—
his infant son falling, a hurtling mass,

and leaping caught him at the bottom stair.)
My daughters! Heaven forbid that I pass
disquiet to you. Pray that I root out
relics of hope from black ruins of doubt.

NOTES

The epigraph is from "Det Öppna Fönstret" / "The Open Window" by Swedish poet / Nobel Laureate Tomas Tranströmer (1931-2015). Translated by Patty Crane in *The Blue House: Collected Works of Tomas Tranströmer* (Copper Canyon Press, 2023), the lines read: "I didn't know which way / to turn my head— / with my visual field divided / like a horse."

"Coming Ashore" engages with an etching by Newfoundland-born artist David Blackwood (1941-2022).

"Weight of the World" engages with a series of photographs snapped in Ukraine for the *Washington Post* by Salwan Georges.

"The Land Agent": "*cum spiritu Hiberneuse*" is a "bog Latin" expression that translates loosely as "in the Irish spirit." Irish playwright Dion Boucicault uses it wittily in his play *The Colleen Bawn* (1860), where his character Myles na Coppaleen explains that it means "wid a keg of poteen" (*poitín* being illegally distilled whiskey).

"*Nuages*," which translates as "Clouds," nods toward a signature tune by manouche guitarist Django Reinhardt (1910-1953) that became an unofficial anthem of the French Resistance during World War II. Reinhardt and violinist Stéphane Grappelli formed the core of the legendary Quintette du Hot Club de France.

"Listening to Josef Locke" engages with the legacy of an Irish tenor, *né* Joseph McLaughlin (1917-1999), who was especially popular during the 1940s and '50s.

"Hermitage": little is known about Bro. S. Ó Maoile, the author of these verses.

"Dizzying" engages with the figure of legendary jazz trumpeter Dizzy Gillespie (1917-1993).

"6 x 6" engages with the playing of a half-dozen wonderful jazz guitarists.

"*This Is My Story, This Is My Song*" engages with an anecdote about legendary jazz pianist Thelonious Monk (1917-1982).

"*The Real Book*" references the series of "fake books" used universally by jazz musicians.

"*Die Mädchen Meiner Träume*" engages with a painting by German expressionist Ernst Ludwig Kirchner (1880-1938).

"*Uaigneas*" is Irish for "loneliness." The gloss following "*Iarmhaireacht*" is from Manchán Magan's *Thirty-Two Words for Field* (Gill Books, 2020).

"Cardigan Days, 1964" recalls an event in the Prince Edward Island village of Cardigan.

"At McNello's": McNello's is a pub in Inniskeen, Co. Monaghan, best known for its association with Irish poet Patrick Kavanagh.

"Paganini": this poem engages with legendary Italian violin virtuoso Niccolò Paganini (1782-1840).

"The Test of the Bow": Irish fiddler Michael Coleman (1891-1945) emigrated from Co. Sligo to New York City in 1918. His recordings continue to influence fiddlers on both sides of the Atlantic.

"After Looking Into R. J. O'Duffy's *Historic Graves in Glasnevin Cemetery* (1915)": the epigraph is from the "Hades" episode of James Joyce's *Ulysses*. The poem remembers Seumas O'Kelly (1881-1918), author of the fine Irish short story "The Weaver's Grave."

ACKNOWLEDGMENTS

The author gratefully acknowledges permission kindly granted by Anita Blackwood, executor of the estate of artist David Blackwood (1941-2022), to use *Coming Ashore* (etching, 1982) for the cover image of this book of poems.

Acknowledgment is given to the following publications in which some of the poems in *Nuages: New Poems* first appeared:

Another Book: "This Is My Story, This Is My Song"

Bookmark at 50: A Commemorative Chapbook: "East Race"

Courier: "The Visitor," "Goldfinch," "Dance of the Seven Plates," "Heron"

The Fiddlehead: "Wheatfield With Crows," "Spuds," "Cardigan Days, 1964"

Fusion: A Magazine of Literature, Music, Art, and Ideas: "The Real Book"

Interdisciplinary Humanities: "6 x 6"

The Poetry Porch: "Wake-up Call," "Turkey Vultures," "Daffodils"

President's Holiday Card, Saint Mary's College: "December Light"

ROAM: "Fledglings"

The "Selected Poems" were previously included in *What Really Matters* (2000) and *Delivering the News* (2019), both published by McGill-Queens University Press in the distinguished Hugh MacLennan Poetry Series. Many of those poems originally appeared in journals acknowledged in those volumes.

BIONOTE

Thomas O'Grady was born and grew up on Prince Edward Island. After a long and rich teaching career at University of Massachusetts Boston, where he was Director of Irish Studies from 1984 to 2019, he relocated to northern Indiana where he is currently Scholar-in-Residence at Saint Mary's College. He now divides his time between and among the banks of the mighty St. Joe River in South Bend, a converted rumrunner's bunkhouse in Adamsville, Rhode Island, and the south shore of his beloved PEI.

The cover of this volume reproduces *Coming Ashore* (1982), an etching by Newfoundland-born artist David Blackwood (1941-2022). This image is used with the kind permission of the Estate of David Blackwood.

Books by

ARROWSMITH
PRESS

Girls by Oksana Zabuzhko

Bula Matari/Smasher of Rocks by Tom Sleigh

This Carrying Life by Maureen McLane

Cries of Animals Dying by Lawrence Ferlinghetti

Animals in Wartime by Matiop Wal

Divided Mind by George Scialabba

The Jinn by Amira El-Zein

Bergstein
edited by Askold Melnyczuk

Arrow Breaking Apart by Jason Shinder

Beyond Alchemy by Daniel Berrigan

Conscience, Consequence: Reflections on Father Daniel Berrigan
edited by Askold Melnyczuk

Ric's Progress by Donald Hall

Return To The Sea by Etnairis Rivera

The Kingdom of His Will by Catherine Parnell

Eight Notes from the Blue Angel by Marjana Savka

Fifty-Two by Melissa Green

Music In—And On—The Air by Lloyd Schwartz

Magpiety by Melissa Green

Reality Hunger by William Pierce

Soundings: On The Poetry of Melissa Green
edited by Sumita Chakraborty

The Corny Toys by Thomas Sayers Ellis

Black Ops by Martin Edmunds

Museum of Silence by Romeo Oriogun

City of Water by Mitch Manning

Passeggiate by Judith Baumel

Persephone Blues by Oksana Lutsyshyna

The Uncollected Delmore Schwartz
edited by Ben Mazer

The Light Outside by George Kovach

The Blood of San Gennaro by Scott Harney
edited by Megan Marshall

No Sign by Peter Balakian

Firebird by Kythe Heller

The Selected Poems of Oksana Zabuzhko
edited by Askold Melnyczuk

The Age of Waiting by Douglas J. Penick

Manimal Woe by Fanny Howe

Crank Shaped Notes by Thomas Sayers Ellis

The Land of Mild Light by Rafael Cadenas
edited by Nidia Hernández

The Silence of Your Name: The Afterlife of a Suicide by Alexandra Marshall

Flame in a Stable by Martin Edmunds

Mrs. Schmetterling by Robin Davidson

This Costly Season by John Okrent

Thorny by Judith Baumel

The Invisible Borders of Time: Five Female Latin American Poets
edited by Nidia Hernández

Some of You Will Know by David Rivard

The Forbidden Door: The Selected Poetry of Lasse Söderberg
tr. by Lars Gustaf Andersson & Carolyn Forché

Unrevolutionary Times by Houman Harouni

Between Fury & Peace: The Many Arts of Derek Walcott
edited by Askold Melnyczuk

The Burning World by Sherod Santos

Today is a Different War: Poetry of Lyudmyla Khersonska
tr. by Olga Livshin, Andrew Janco, Maya Chhabra, & Lev Fridman

ARROWSMITH is named after the late William Arrowsmith, a renowned classics scholar, literary and film critic. General editor of thirty-three volumes of *The Greek Tragedy in New Translations*, he was also a brilliant translator of Eugenio Montale, Cesare Pavese, and others. Arrowsmith, who taught for years in Boston University's University Professors Program, championed not only the classics and the finest in contemporary literature, he was also passionate about the importance of recognizing the translator's role in bringing the original work to life in a new language.

Like the arrowsmith who turns his arrows straight and true,
a wise person makes his character straight and true.

— Buddha

www.ingramcontent.com/pod-product-compliance
Lightning Source LLC
Chambersburg PA
CBHW021207130626
46554CB00005B/2025